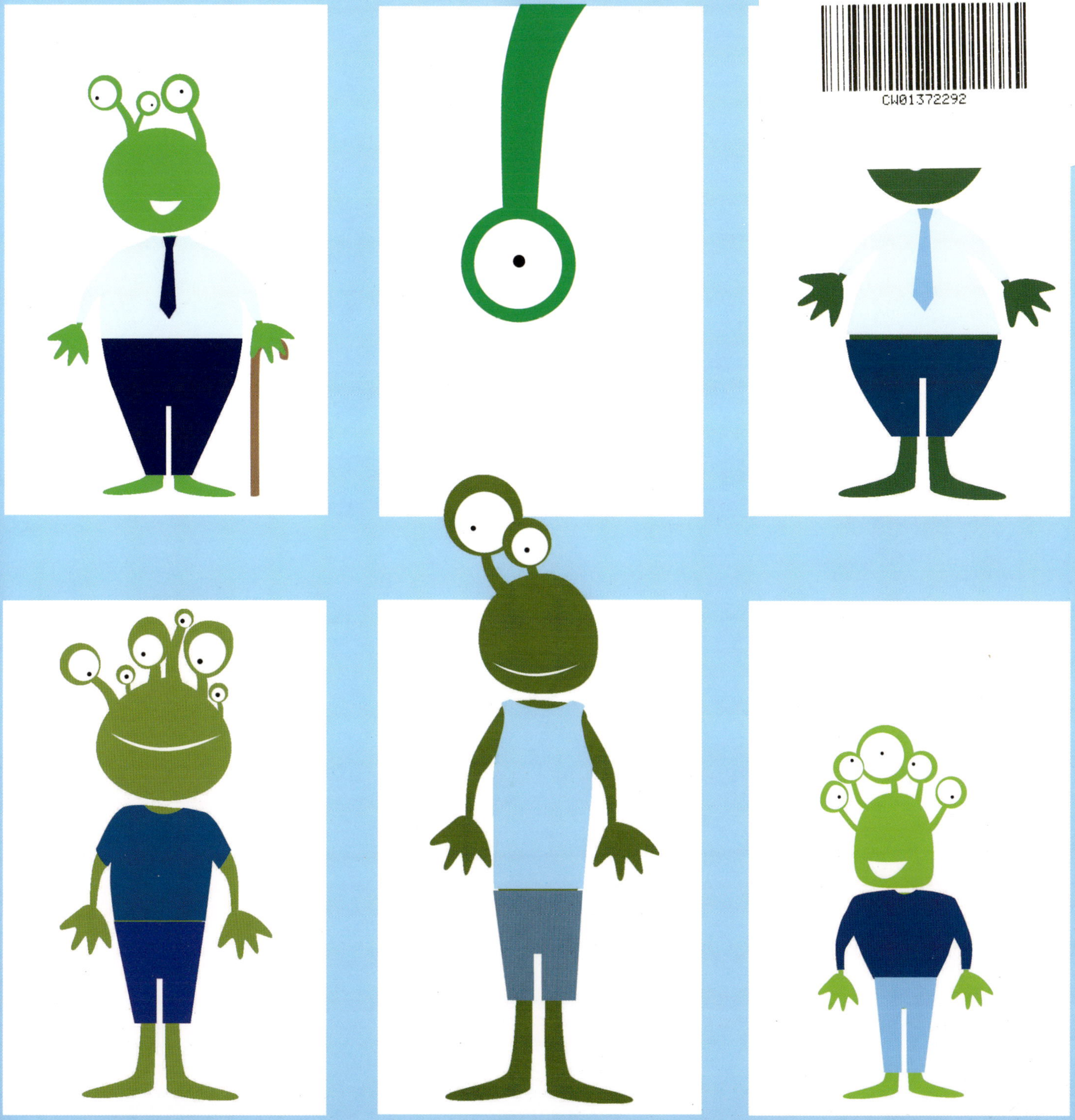

First published in 2017
by The Proud Trust
49/51 Sidney Street
Manchester
M1 7HB UK
Second impression January 2018.

Text, design and illustrations copyright © The Proud Trust 2017.

All rights reserved. No part of this publication may be reproduced
or transmitted by any means, electronic, mechanical, photocopying
or otherwise, without the prior permission of the publisher.

ISBN 978-0-9957394-0-6
Printed and bound in the UK.

Written by Matty Donaldson
Design by Lucy Harding
Illustrations by Sarah Fisher and Lucy Harding
Co-edited by Rachel Williams

Supporting educational resources for schools and teachers can be found here

www.theproudtrust.org/alien-nation

This book is dedicated to all the gender explorers out there who are creating new spaces for us to exist in, and new possibilities for us to be.

The creation of Alien Nation was very much a collaborative labour of love. Special thanks are extended to all the trans and non-binary young people that gave their time and so much of themselves in the development of this story:

Arthur
Chris
Charlie
Ezekiel
Frankie
Jordyn
Natalie
Noah
Rain
Sky
Taylor
Zach

Special Thank You

You are all fabulous and glorious!

OUR
STORY
STARTS
DEEP
DEEP
DEEP
DEEP
DEEP IN OUT

ER **SPACE,**
in a galaxy far, far away.

In this galaxy there lived

a group of aliens.

Ask What noises do aliens make?

These aliens lived

on two planets.

The first planet was Planet Girl. **EVERYTHING** on Planet Girl was pink. The sky was pink, the trees were pink, even the birds were pink!

Everyone who was sent to live on Planet Girl had to follow the Planet Girl rules

- MUST like pink
- MUST wear dresses
- MUST be feminine

ASK
Can you think of any more rules that they might have on Planet Girl?
How do you feel about these rules?
Why do you think they have these rules?

The second planet was Planet Boy. **EVERYTHING** on Planet Boy was blue. The clouds were blue, the streets were blue, and everyone lived in a blue house!

Everyone who was sent to live on Planet Boy had to follow the Planet Boy rules

- MUST like blue
- MUST wear trousers
- MUST be masculine

ASK Can you think of any more rules that they might have on Planet Boy?
How do you feel about these rules?
Why do you think they have these rules?

When the baby aliens were born, the Alien Leader felt that they needed a way to decide whether to send them to live on Planet Girl or Planet Boy.

Planet Girl.

The Leader decided that all the baby aliens who were blue would be boys, and they were sent to Planet Boy.

When it came to the aliens who were more red or turquoise or purple, the Leader would guess if the baby alien

was closer to pink

or closer to blue.

Of course, the Leader would sometimes get it wrong!

They sometimes got it wrong because all of the baby aliens were beautiful and unique, and didn't fit neatly into just two groups.

They sometimes got it wrong because they chose where the aliens belonged, rather than letting the aliens decide for themselves.

And... They sometimes got it wrong because they thought that the aliens' bodies could tell us something about what the alien would be like when they were older.

As time went on, the baby aliens grew

As they grew up, they began to explore who they were and where they belonged.

Lots of the aliens on Planet Girl were really happy, and they felt like they belonged there.

The only thing they didn't like were THE RULES.

They would look across to Planet Boy and wonder why they were allowed to do things differently.

"Why should we have to like pink?

Why should we have to wear dresses?

Why should we have to be feminine (whatever that means anyway)?

Why can't we do what we want to do, and be who we want to be?"

So one day all the aliens on Planet Girl got together. They got hold of the rules,

they ripped them up

and all the aliens cheered and celebrated!

Ask What types of things do girls get told they CAN'T do, or MUST do?
What do you think about this?

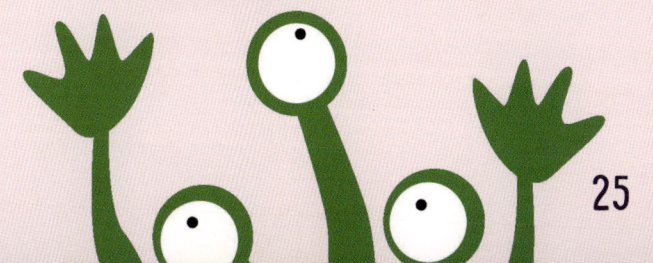

25

However, there was a group of aliens who didn't feel like they belonged there. Even though they no longer had to like pink, or wear dresses, or be feminine (whatever that means anyway), they knew that they didn't feel comfortable on Planet Girl.

Some of them knew that they really belonged on Planet Boy, and some of them weren't comfortable being on either planet.
The leader had got it wrong.

Ask How do you think these aliens felt being sent to the wrong planet?

Lots of the aliens on Planet Boy were really happy, and they felt like they belonged there.

The only thing they didn't like were THE RULES.

They would look across to Planet Girl and wonder why they were allowed to do things differently.

"Why should we have to like blue?

Why should we have to wear only trousers?

Why should we have to be masculine (whatever that means anyway)?

Why can't we do what we want to do and be who we want to be?"

So one day all the aliens on Planet Boy got together.
They got hold of the rules,

they ripped them up

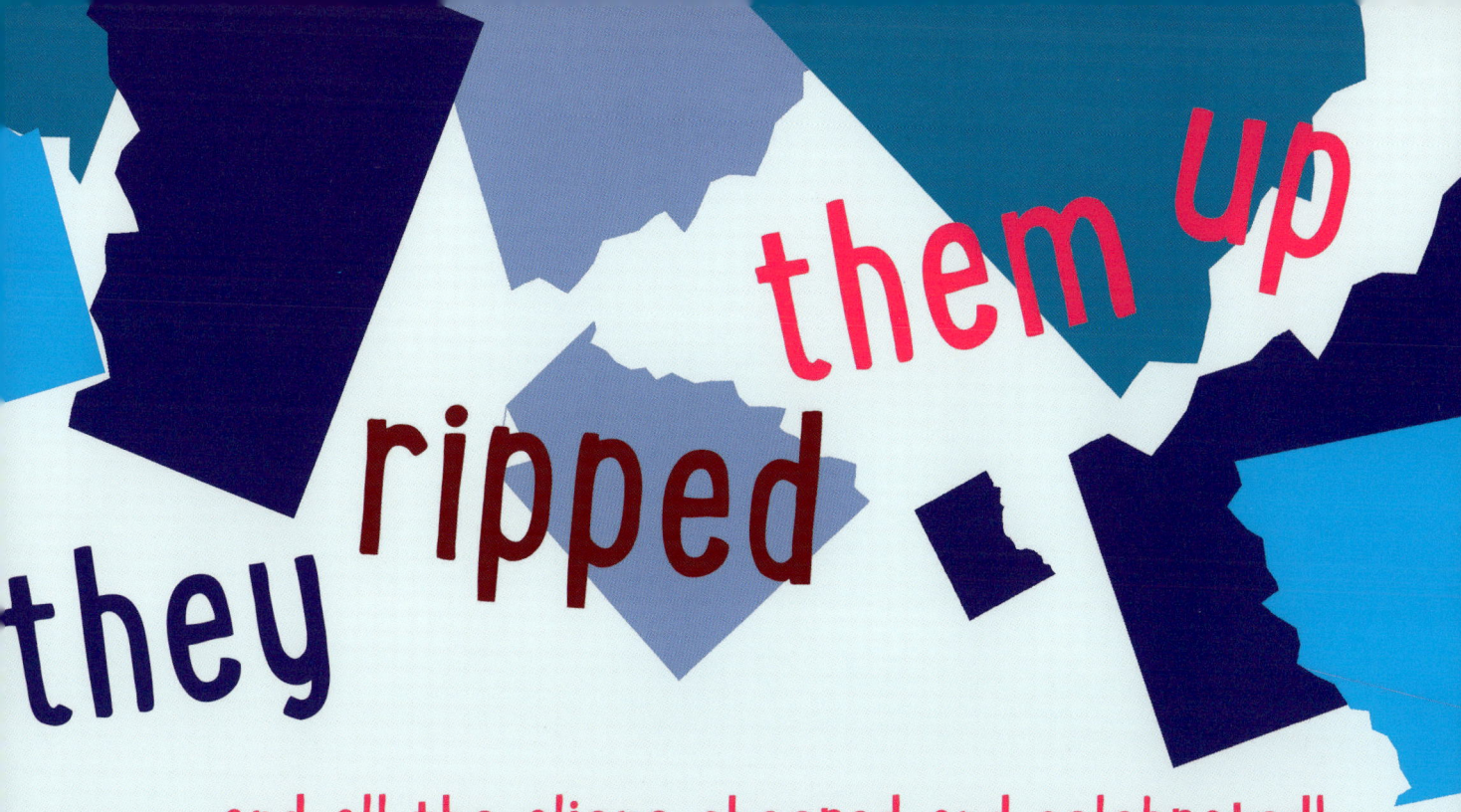

and all the aliens cheered and celebrated!

Ask What types of things do boys get told they CAN'T do, or MUST do?
What do you think about this?

31

However, there was a group of aliens who felt like they didn't belong there. Even though they no longer had to like blue, or wear trousers, or be masculine (whatever that means anyway) they knew that they didn't feel comfortable on Planet Boy.

Some of them knew that they really belonged on Planet Girl, and some of them weren't comfortable being on either planet. The leader had got it wrong again!

Ask How do you think these aliens felt being sent to the wrong planet?

POWER TO THE ~~PEOPLE~~ ALIENS

The aliens who had been sent to the wrong planet started to find each other and form groups together.

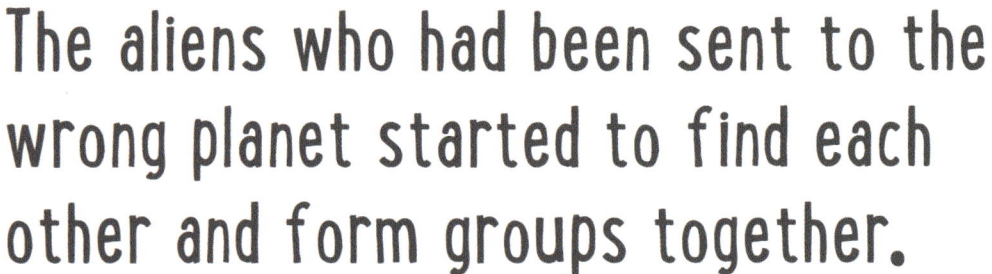

MARCH LIKE **MARTIN** SPEAK LIKE **MALCOLM**

Free Cee Cee

HE

THEY

HE

RESPECT PRONOUNS

"We must do something," they said.

When the Alien Leader heard about the situation, they felt terrible that they had sent these aliens to live on the wrong planets. They said...

It's not good enough that MOST of my aliens are happy. I want ALL of my aliens to be happy. We must do something!

A meeting was called on the Leader's spaceship to try to come up with a plan of what to do. They thought and they thought and they thought some more. Just as they were about to give up hope a determined voice rose up from the back.

She said...

Why don't we build a bridge between the two planets?

All the aliens thought that this was an excellent idea.

39

So the aliens started to build.

They built

and they built

until they

could

feel their arms.

barely

during the night.

and they built

during the day

They built

Until one day...

The bridge was finished!

All of the aliens

cheered and celebrated!

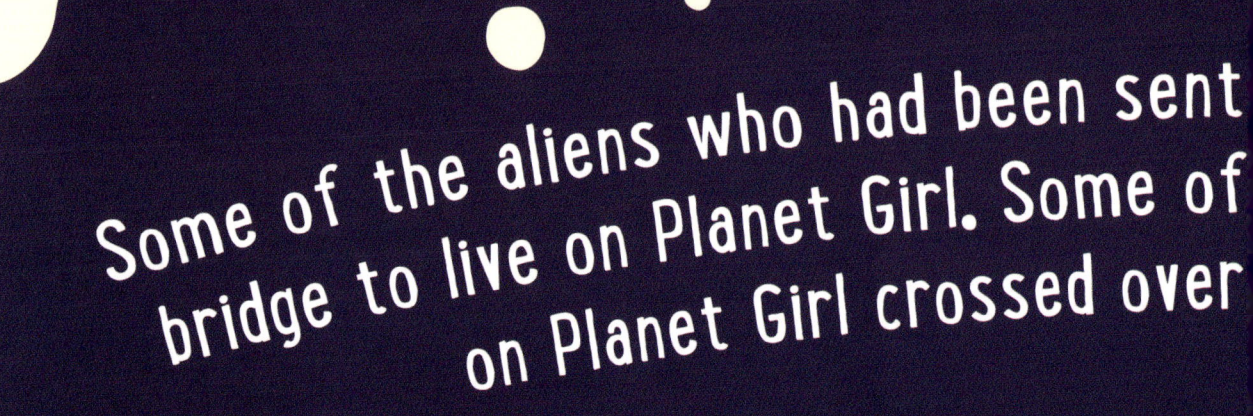

Some of the aliens who had been sent bridge to live on Planet Girl. Some of on Planet Girl crossed over

Some of the aliens took their time with the crossing.

Some of them

to live on Planet Boy crossed over the the aliens who had been sent to live the bridge to live on Planet Boy.

ran straight over.

While some aliens tried both planets before deciding where to live.

There was also a group of aliens who felt like they didn't belong on either planet, but somewhere else. This is because they didn't really feel like a girl or a boy. They felt like something else, something just as important.

I feel like I'm a girl and a boy

Some of these aliens would move fluidly, spending time on the bridge as well as on both of the planets.

I don't feel like a girl or a boy

THEY

However, some of them decided to build another planet for themselves, and for other aliens who were not girls or boys, but something else, something just as important.

The aliens came up with words to help describe what was happening:

★ CIS ★ The aliens who stayed on the planet they had been sent to called themselves cis, because cis means "on the same side".

>>> TRANS

The aliens who crossed over the bridge to live on another planet called themselves trans, because trans means "to cross over".

NON-BINARY

The aliens who lived on the third planet, or who wandered between planets, called themselves non-binary. Non-binary is a word that can describe those who don't feel like a girl or a boy, or who feel like both.

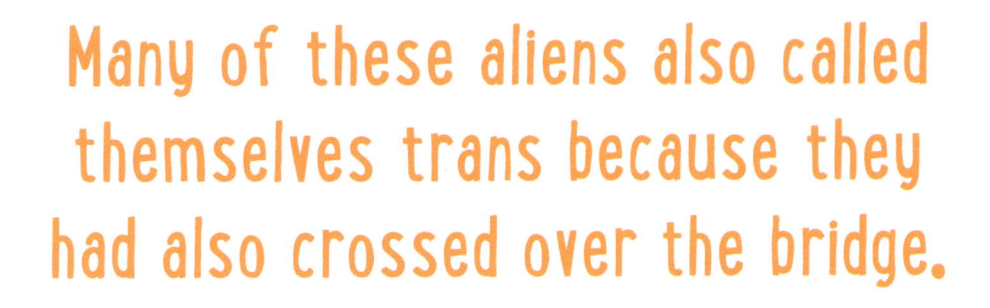

Many of these aliens also called themselves trans because they had also crossed over the bridge.

Lots of aliens used other words to describe themselves.

ASK What words do you use to describe who you are?

All of the aliens were much happier.

Even though some aliens still insisted that 'girls things' and 'boys things' existed, the rules had been ripped up, so the aliens were free to ignore this.

And even though some of the aliens struggled to understand those who were different to them, they were learning and starting to be friends.

And even though the Alien Leader still sent alien babies to Planet Girl or Planet Boy when they were born, they could now move freely between the planets and be comfortable with who they are.

They knew they still had a long way to go before things would be perfect, but for now they were better and that was worth **CELEBRATING.**

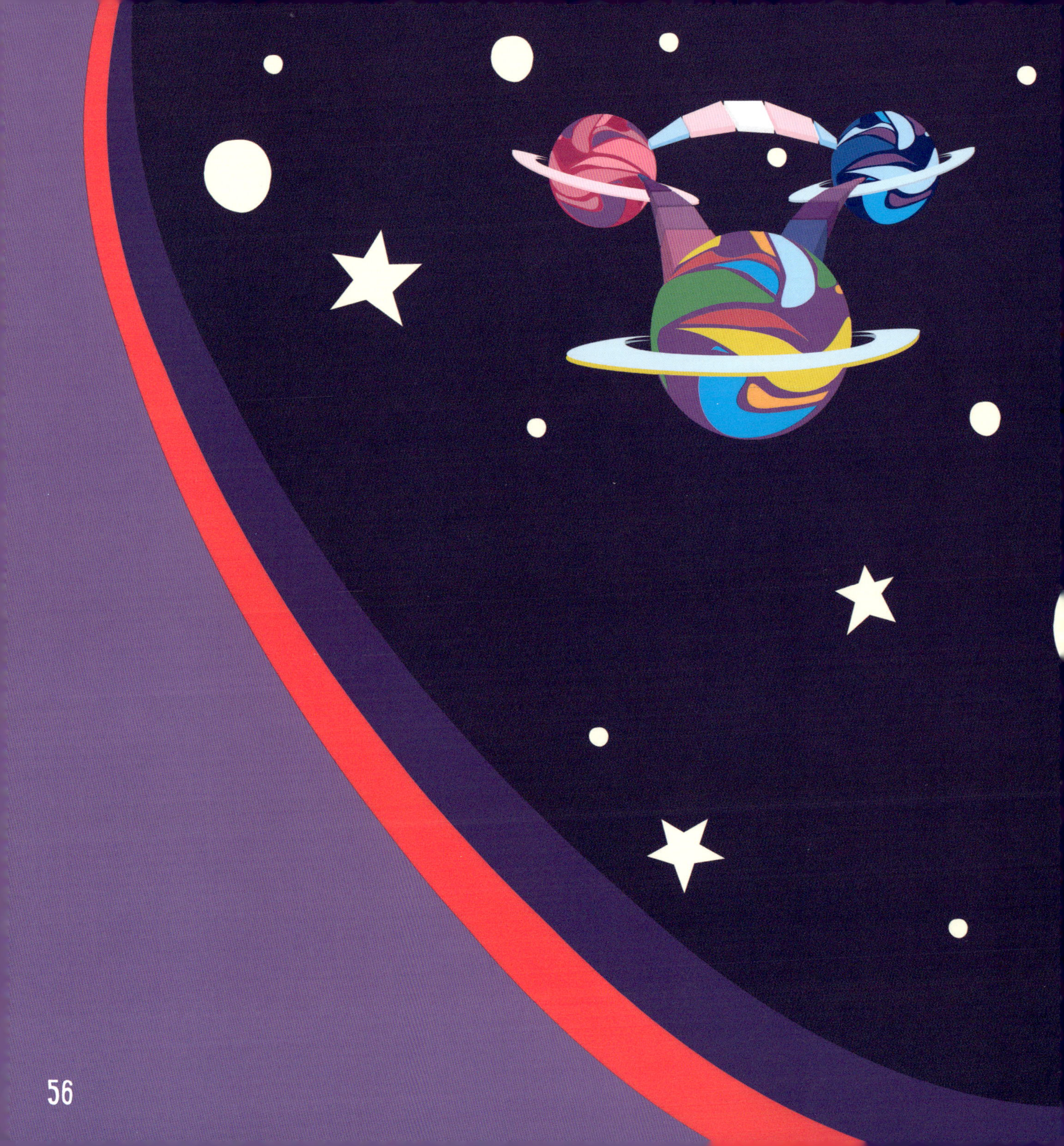

THE END

...or is it just the beginning?

Acknowledgments

Thanks to more than 100 trans and non-binary young people who gave their time and voices to the story, you know who you are.

Thanks to all the staff at The Proud Trust and to close friends. You listened to us talk about aliens non-stop for a year, but you also helped to shape the story as it is today. Also thank you to Hebe Phillips for her original styling contribution.

Thanks to the primary schools who let us trial the story and to the children who listened to the earlier versions. Also to the primary teachers that have shown great enthusiasm towards the book and helped us create the supporting educational resources.

Thanks to Cheshire West and Chester Council for funding the development of the project and allowing Alien Nation to become a reality.

the PROUD Trust
home of LGBT+ youth

The Proud Trust is a lifesaving and life enhancing organisation, that helps LGBT+ young people to empower themselves, to make a positive change for themselves and their communities.

Supporting educational resources for schools and teachers can be found here

www.theproudtrust.org/alien-nation

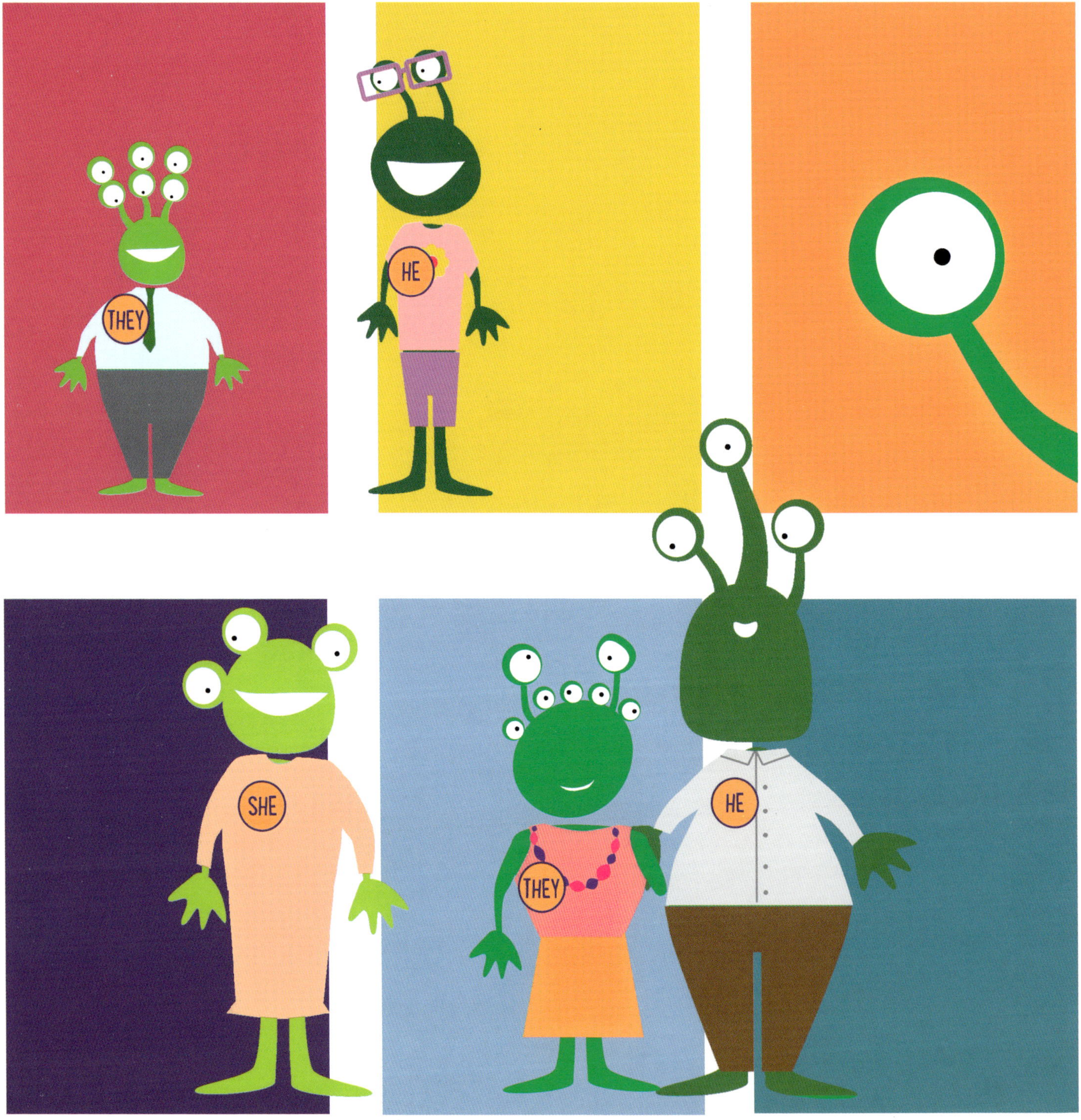
THEY
HE
SHE
THEY
HE